CW00517415

This notebook belongs to:

....

If lost, please contact:

....

Sharing know-how
Building *will* and skill
Working together

©Notebook Mentor First Edition 2019
Practical help and guidance through
meaningful work and career experiences

To shop online or find out more go to
www.notebookmentor.com

Designed by Joe Hales studio
Printed and bound in Belgium by Graphius

Notebook Mentor takes sustainability seriously.
Our products are printed and sourced
responsibly. We check the credibility of our
supply chain partners and carry out annual
audits to monitor and achieve our sustainability
goals.

British Library Cataloguing in Publication data.
A catalogue record for the book is available
from the British Library.

ISBN 978-1-913389-01-7

Getting On

The 1st 90 days
in my new job

About Notebook Mentor Founder and Author

Elisa Nardi is a highly respected Human Resources (HR) expert, business executive, author and mentor. She has spent over three decades immersed in the corporate world, nearly half as a Chief HR Officer responsible for *people*. By her reckoning, she has dealt with literally thousands of people based work experiences across the entire employee lifecycle – from hire to retire. Elisa has been exposed to positive situations at work such as nurturing young talent, coaching managers and empowering teams, to helping those in personal crisis or going through significant organisational change. In fact, dealing sensitively with demanding change and transformation has been the hallmark of Elisa's career.

In 2015 Elisa momentarily blacked out, badly broke both wrists and was diagnosed with a brain tumour. She had double wrist and life-saving brain surgery shortly after. Although she returned to her corporate role for a further two years, Elisa recognised that the experience had changed her. It also fuelled her interest in the brain – in neuroscience or the biology of the mind. Elisa is fascinated by how the brain takes in information, learns, remembers and makes sense of the world. For good reason, she recognises the need to allow the brain time to process the constant stream of everyday experience. She is fascinated by how we can problem solve and learn using all our senses (especially balancing visual, auditory and kinaesthetic), reflecting and giving ourselves space to reconcile what we are facing with what we already know.

These passions, combined with a deep love of physical notebooks, led to the creation of Notebook Mentor – practical help and guidance workbooks and online support resources to help you through meaningful work and career experiences.

Elisa is the Founder of Notebook Mentor and CEO of ēniteō limited, a small HR consulting and mentoring business. She holds honours degrees in both Psychology and Sociology and is qualified to use numerous psychometric tools and methodologies. She holds the Institute of Leadership and Management Executive Mentoring and Coaching qualification from Oxford Brookes. Elisa was appointed to the Board of the British Medical Association in 2019, as independent non-executive director.

Contents

1

Chapter 1

Introducing Notebook Mentor

"Discontent is the first necessity of progress"

Thomas Edison

Mentoring

Simply put mentoring can be described as *someone helping you out*. This *someone* is a person who has knowledge or experience of a subject of interest to you and is willing to share their know-how, such that you can learn from it and use it to develop or better manage your situation. Done well it is different from someone offering you more general advice or giving you their opinion – however well-intentioned!

Mentoring takes many forms. It can be informal and brief – such as an expert giving you advice via a TED Talk, or more formal and longer-term – such as a leader in business supporting you in a transition to a new, more senior role. It can also take the form of reverse mentoring – when a more junior individual with expert knowledge offers advice to a senior person unskilled in the same area.

Mentoring can help you build a skill or support you through a period of uncertainty and change. It can give you the confidence to face a difficult challenge or lean into an unexpected opportunity. It can help stimulate ideas about what actions to take or which path to choose. By encouraging reflection and working on your capacity to solve problems, one possible outcome of mentoring is that it can help you arrive at high-quality decisions, faster.

The aim of mentoring is to help you become more capable and motivated to manage your situation or development on a continual basis. Effective mentoring builds ability and encourages the desire for independence and self-reliance, even if this takes time. A mentoring experience should help you emerge wiser, more confident and informed about how to tackle whatever it is you are facing.

Notebook mentoring

Notebook mentoring is an accessible and cost-effective alternative to the more traditional forms of mentoring found in the workplace. We provide mentoring through our physical notebooks, supported by other visual and auditory resources. Our mentoring is based on:

- Sharing our expert know-how and experience, whilst
- Engaging you in reflective practice and personal inquiry,
- Allowing you to apply restraint, perspective and judgement to your situation.

In doing so we help you not only build the *skill* to manage your experience but the *will* to continuously learn and move forward.

We only use experts in the subject matter to write our notebooks. All have decades of experience and come from professional backgrounds in business, psychology or HR. They have faced or guided others through situations just like this one.

Our notebooks cover topics typically experienced from the beginning to the end of your working life. These topics are grouped under different category headings such as Getting Started, Getting On, Managing Others, Leading, When Things Don't Go To Plan and Life Transitions. More titles are being added regularly. Please check out the website for the latest updates by visiting **www.notebookmentor.com**

Think of each Notebook Mentor as a *working document* and your concentration on the subject as *work in progress*. While we offer you guidance on how to pace your mentoring experience, you will be able to take charge of when and for how long you focus on the issues, challenges and opportunities at hand and whether you return to a section of the notebook many times over.

Meaningful work and career experiences

Maybe you are starting a new job, becoming a manager for the first time or are trying to balance your work and life? Perhaps you are facing a life-changing event like starting a family or you are dealing with a stress-related illness? Your department might be under restructure or perhaps you are simply not getting on with someone at work? Maybe you want to understand yourself better or are taking on new responsibilities you've never had before? These situations and experiences are meaningful and they can happen across the lifespan of your work and career.

Meaningful experiences can be life-affirming, positive and exciting, equally they can be destructive, negative and painful. As an individual, you decide how a specific moment makes you feel, even if that's different from how someone else experiences the same moment.

Meaningful experiences can also have a radiating impact on other aspects of your life, on how you think and feel. While our notebooks focus on a specific topic you will always find that we try to look at the topic as holistically as possible, considering the 'impact spread'.

Multi-sensory learning

Notebook Mentors connection to the physical craft of *thinking* and *writing* is informed by both a love of printed notebooks and an on-going fascination with the human brain – with how you take in information, reflect and process it, seize opportunities and take action.

You learn and process information in a **multi-sensory way** – smell, taste, visually (by sight), in an auditory way (by hearing) and kinaesthetically (through touch). Notebook Mentor encourages this multi-sensory approach, combining **visual learning** (like reading this notebook or viewing our website) with **auditory learning** (for example listening to a relevant podcast or talking to a colleague about the Notebook Mentor experience) and **kinaesthetic learning** (in this instance the physical art of writing in our notebooks). We think the best learning happens when you actively engage using these three modalities, rather than just one or two. It is this last modality – kinaesthetic learning, that has become less relevant in a connected, technology-led age. It's an imbalance we want to address.

To learn from your experience and align your behaviour to your goals you need to allow your brain introspective time to reconcile new information with prior experience. You also need information, thoughts, reflections and ideas to stick in your long-term memory. Notebook Mentor uses reflective practice, personal inquiry, restraint, perspective and judgement to help you look back, understand and deal with what is happening in the moment *and* manage priorities and create breakthrough ideas for a better future.

At Notebook Mentor we recognise that our audience is likely to be largely adult. As an adult, we want to collaborate with you – not simply tell you what to do. We respect your prior experience and how this might influence the way you learn (or indeed unlearn) something. Put all this together and learning becomes relevant, meaningful and despite a challenge, enjoyable.

Using Notebook Mentor to help manage a particular life experience can be relevant and orientated (though not exclusively) to problem-solving. We recognise, however, that not all things are problems to solve. We therefore, hope to pique your curiosity to progress to mastery of your situation – whatever that may be. Notebook Mentor is here to help you make the most of the opportunities that present themselves and to support you to prepare for, navigate through and learn from the moments that are difficult and distracting. By sharing our expert know-how, and through your partnership in completing the exercises that guide, test and challenge you, together we build your *will* and *skill* to get you the outcomes you want.

You are not alone in this

Developing skills and traits

If we were beginning our mentoring relationship face to face the first thing we would do is get to know one another. This would help build rapport and empathy, which in turn would help us have deep and open conversations. Having empathy is another way of saying that we can tune into others at an emotional level. For this form of mentoring the most important relationship is the one you have with yourself. This means spending quality time with your thoughts, having those same open and deep conversations. This requires the ability to tune in to you. To help you tune in to you, Notebook Mentor requires you to undertake **reflective practice** and **personal inquiry.** Reflective practice is a structured technique to help you study your experience and the thoughts and feelings that arise as a result. By evaluating and analysing experiences you can draw conclusions and be planful about any actions required. Personal inquiry requires you to ask important questions about yourself – about the type of person you are and want to be. In addition, we will encourage you to think about **personal restraint, perspective and judgement**. Restraint simply asks that you hold back or hold the space 'open' for a moment giving your brain time to process experience. Perspective asks you to look broadly, connecting the dots, considering a variety of views. And judgement means applying logic *and* instinct to thinking smartly. All are essential for creativity and problem-solving.

To make best use of your Notebook Mentor it's worth you being mindful of the traps and pitfalls that can get in the way of your success or slow you down. So in Chapter 2 of every notebook, we encourage you to briefly assess your previous experience (or not) of mentoring and whether this could help or hinder you. In Chapter 3 of every notebook, we ask you to practise the skills and traits mentioned above. Think of it as a warm-up to the deeper conversations that are to come. Whether you are new to Notebook Mentor or have used our notebooks before try not to skip Chapters 2 and 3. The content may not immediately feel relevant to the subject at hand but in time we hope you will revisit your reflections and add to your analysis. Chapter 3, in particular, has the potential to become a narrative or story for describing who you are.

We encourage you to continue using other valuable support mechanisms that may already be working for you such as members of your family, your doctor, a work colleague or friend. And be kind to yourself by giving yourself time to enjoy the mentoring experience.

2

Chapter 2

Your mentoring history

We cannot see our reflection in running water. It is only in still water that we can see.

Zen Proverb

Mentoring experience

You most likely receive some sort of help and guidance every day. Sometimes it's useful and at other times it can be delivered badly, in a rush and when you least expect or want it! Let's face it everyone loves to give advice. From partners, parents, your children, your boss, work colleagues or friends on social media – it's one experience people tend to have in common.

Recent experience or memories from the past can help or hinder a new experience like Notebook Mentor, so let's start by answering a straight forward but important question.

Building will and skill

◆ Why did you buy this Notebook Mentor? (If someone else bought it, why do you think they did so?)

◆ What are your thoughts and feelings about mentoring?

_____

_____

_____

_____

_____

_____

_____

◆ Have you had any formal mentoring or support, like coaching, before? If yes, when was it and how did it come about?

_____

_____

_____

_____

_____

_____

_____

◆ If you have experienced mentoring previously (or some other form or tutored advice) – what worked well and not so well?

....

....

....

....

....

....

....

◆ If you have never experienced mentoring before, what do you imagine it to be?

....

....

....

....

....

....

....

◆ What are your hopes and/or fears of experiencing a mentoring process?

◆ What conclusions (if any) do you draw about how Notebook Mentor might work for you? Do you foresee any hurdles you might need to overcome to make the experience useful? How might you overcome them?

TIP
Answer these questions but also let them 'sit with you'. Reflect on them when your mind has a chance to wander and go where it pleases (perhaps on a train or bus journey, as you relax in the bath, walk the dog or sit in the garden)

Sharing know-how

We hope you bought this Notebook Mentor because you are open to learning and are interested in being helped and supported. If someone bought the notebook for you then we are guessing that they care about you and want to help you manage a meaningful experience, without simply resorting to giving you their opinion. That's pretty thoughtful of them. Whatever the reason – because you feel challenged, because you want help, because you are excited, because you've decided to spend quality time on yourself – taking the first step on any journey is a positive start – congratulations.

If you have been lucky enough to experience any kind of mentoring before, we do hope you had a positive experience. There are many benefits to mentoring.

It can:

- Help you get clear about what you are aiming for
- Help you find the motivation to tackle something, grow or personally develop
- Encourage reflection, inquiry, restraint, perspective and judgement
- Develop skills and personal attributes that make you more employable
- Support improvement in your performance
- Build personal confidence in a safe, supported, private environment
- Help you get noticed (if that's what you want)

And the benefits aren't just for you:

- More inquisitive, thoughtful thinkers help creativity and innovation to flourish
- Sharing skills and knowledge helps an organisation to learn
- When done in this way, it's cost-effective

If you have been traditionally mentored before and felt negative about it there are some reasons why it might not have worked for you:

- There was insufficient time set aside to make it work
- The process was or became too superficial

- One or other of the party distrusted the motive or goals of the other
- The rapport that you once felt disappeared
- Your mentor was too autocratic or judgemental about you

This can happen for different reasons and it's worth acknowledging this now, either parking it (recognising that it happened in the past and you are now trying something different), or if you are able, let go of any negative thoughts and feelings.

If you have never experienced mentoring before then we are delighted that you have an opportunity to give this type of support and guidance a go. It may work for you brilliantly or you may feel it's not for you. Take your time, read the content carefully and work through the exercises at your own pace. Our experience suggests that when it comes to mentoring people are often looking for:

- A sounding board – someone who will challenge assumptions or ideas
- An inspirer or motivator to encourage reflection and action
- Support that is non-judgemental
- A credible expert or role model

This enables you to:

- Practice, evaluate and adapt in a thoughtful, less exposed way
- Grow your confidence and competence
- Enhance your self-awareness, self-evaluation and interpersonal skills
- Become autonomous

Notebook Mentor is here to help you test and learn. We nudge you to complete exercises that challenge assumptions you may have and help you develop your ideas and thinking. We encourage you to reflect and act with inquiry, restraint, perspective and the application of judgement – in a non-critical and supportive way. We bring credible expertise, thought-leadership and experience to subjects of real interest to real people.

The Notebook Mentor team gets immense satisfaction from helping people from all walks of life and in a vast array of different jobs get practical help and guidance through meaningful work experiences.

3

Chapter 3

Tuning into you

"Knowing yourself is the beginning of all wisdom"

Aristotle

Knowing yourself (or developing self-awareness)

If you are to learn through this mentoring process it is important that you know yourself or are self-aware. Psychologist Daniel Goleman (1998) defined self-awareness as "the ability to recognize and understand your moods, emotions, and drivers, as well as their effect on others". Being self-aware is about knowing who you *were* in the past and who you *are* today. Your experiences shape how you react to the world around you. Reflecting on the world around you is therefore also part of building self-awareness. It is the cornerstone for developing emotional intelligence.

But where to start?

Let's start by seeing how well you know yourself and how easy it is for you to reflect on who you are. Think about you as a whole person – at work, at home, at play. Don't feel constrained or ponder the questions for too long – just be true to what you write and don't worry if you find this section hard.

If you get stuck have a look at **'Sharing know-how'** at the end of this section for some clues and guidance.

Building will and skill

What are you like? Write down any words that say something about you? They could be words that come to mind in your head. They might be taken from your CV or be words others have used to describe you. They could be words you have or are using on social media or they could even be found by looking at pictures of you – any source will do.

 Don't feel self-conscious or constrained and write as much as you feel is necessary to capture a written picture of who you are. Use the blank notebook section if you run out of room here, and remember to let ideas sit with you for a while, returning to these pages in due course.

"The best way to predict your future is to create it"

Abraham Lincoln

◆ What do you like doing – work-wise, socially, alone, with friends, family, colleagues?

....

....

....

....

....

....

....

◆ What do you dislike? What do find hard, what irritates, tires you, frustrates you?

....

....

....

....

....

....

....

....

◆ How have you changed over the last 5 years? (5 years is an arbitrary choice of time so if it makes more sense to look at 10 years or 2 years that's just fine).

For example, you could describe changes in your appearance, newly learnt skills or knowledge, experiences you have been through or the jobs you have done.

◆ What have been the most significant events you have experienced or been through in the past? (For example, starting a new job, leaving a job, completing an important project or achieving a work goal, getting married, losing a parent or someone dear to you, starting a relationship, ending a relationship, moving house – anything small or large that was a significant experience).

List up to 10 things:

◆ 1 ....

....

◆ 2 ....

....

◆ 3 ....

....

◆ 4 ....

....

◆ 5 ....

....

◆ 6

◆ 7

◆ 8

◆ 9

◆ 10

◆ Let your mind detach and wander – when looking at these events what thoughts and feelings come to mind?

◆ In what way might the events you outlined previously be impacting you today? Is the impact positive or negative?

◆ What do your answers to the previous questions say about your current situation? Can you conclude anything from them? Have they prompted you to take any action? If so, what?

Sharing know-how

Let's begin by asking a basic question – why do we want you to answer questions about yourself and your experiences?

Answer – to be able to answer questions about yourself and your experiences means you are consciously working on knowing yourself or your self-awareness! It takes reflection, inquiry, restraint, perspective and judgment – all the skills we want to help you build. All skills that will help you problem-solve and get creative.

At this stage, we are just starting to explore who you are. Congratulations if you found it easy to answer the questions. If however, like many people we have met, you found it hard, read on for some useful tips.

Finding the right words

Finding words to describe who you are might sound easy – just look to the Oxford English Dictionary where there are thousands of describing words that could be relevant.

But that's just the point. Which words are truly relevant to you? You are a unique person – even those who have shared a similar upbringing and schooling to you do not share your every experience. Your nature and nurture make you unique. It's therefore likely that the words you use will be unique to you.

Which few really capture the nub or essence of who you are? Which few have endured over time? Which few are words you use to describe yourself as well as words others use to describe you?

In no particular order here are just a few describing words that may or may not be meaningful to you. Go back to the questions and if it makes sense to do so apply some of these – find your own if they don't quite fit.

Analytical	**Logical**	**Spirited**	**Thoughtful**
Kind	**Creative**	**Sensible**	**Healthy**
Intense	**Caring**	**Wise**	**Ponderous**
Helpful	**Comic**	**Angry**	**Happy**

Optimistic	Driven	Energetic	Sad
Strategic	Funny	Tactical	Grateful
Ambitious	Trusting	Careful	Challenging
Ego free	Numerate	Bashful	Quiet
Outgoing	Social	Fun-loving	Operational
Musical	Innovative	Unhappy	Confused
Colorful	Down to earth	Conceptual	Commercial
Engaging	Shy	Passionate	Detailed
Courageous	Committed	Demanding	Critical
Cool	Mindful	Reluctant	Quirky
Individual	Miserable	Goofy	Team-orientated
Level headed	Loving	Calm	Accountable
Nice	Punctual	Dutiful	Expressive
Objective	Sincere	Tense	Timid
Welcoming	Loyal	Collegiate	Reliable
Forgiving	Humorous	Inquiring	Jovial
Powerful	Quick	Warm	Athletic
Brave	Bold	Sarcastic	Smart
Intellectual	Practical	Hands-on	Casual
Political	Nervous	Lonely	Comfortable
Soft	Gregarious	Artistic	Grounded
Adventurous	Carefree	Leader	Partner
Pessimistic	Frustrated	Sporty	Sullen

We could go on... **and yes we recognize that many of these words may at first appear positively or negatively loaded**. Being 'angry' isn't something you are likely to aspire to. Being 'caring' sounds very nice. The point is not to judge what their meaning is to others, but to judge how right they feel for you *at this moment*. It just might be that right now the thing that describes you best is 'angry'. That's ok – know your starting point.

> **TIP**
> If you have generated lots of words about the type of company you work for, the job that you do or the hobbies that you have – that's fine but do try and put them in the context of what they say about 'who you are and how you operate'.

Knowing what you like and dislike is useful personal inquiry. It can inform why you have described yourself in a certain way. It can give clues to your interests, perhaps your natural skills and abilities, certainly your motivation for things.

Taking the time to analyze and evaluate your experience helps you understand how your current ideas and beliefs about the world might have formed. When new information confirms your ideas and beliefs as 'correct' you feel comfortable and positive. Sometimes, however, new information challenges your assumptions – you realize that perhaps you were wrong about something. This can lead to what psychologists and educationalists call 'cognitive conflict'. To move forward and be productive you must reconcile your prior ideas and beliefs to this new information. This requires you to constructively deal with the conflict to move forward.

Everybody goes through *meaningful experiences at work*. These significant moments can be positive and uplifting, they can also be hard, demoralizing, draining or sad. Sometimes they can be a combination of good and bad. When you are tackling something interesting or significant, recognizing how your past and current experience has or is shaping you is an important reflection. It certainly has the potential to help or hinder how you now behave and react going forward.

The 'so what' factor?

It's early in our mentoring relationship and already you should have completed lots of reflection. Maybe the 'so what?' question is already buzzing around your head – why am I doing this? When am I going to be told to go and do something?

The answer, perhaps frustratingly, is straightforward:

Q. Why am I doing this?
A. We've already clearly stated the reason for needing to get into reflection and inquiry. Go back and re-read Section 1!

Q. When am I actually going to be told to go and do something?
A. At this stage, we are not suggesting you have to 'do something' with your reflection. Hold the 'space' open and keep inquiring. If an action naturally comes to mind that is helpful to you, by all means, implement it.

We hope that looking back you might already feel that the work completed so far has helped you:

- Know yourself a little better
- Understand what you like and dislike
- Describe yourself to others using words that have meaning to you
- Get prepared for talking about yourself to others – for example, that all-important job interview
- Think about what might be holding you back.

The key is that you are learning reflective practice, personal inquiry, restraint, perspective and judgment and these are traits and skills worth having in their own right without a forward agenda on which to apply them.

It's now time to look into the meaningful experience you are facing and the topic of this notebook.

4

Chapter 4

The 1st 90 days in my new job

You don't have to have it all figured out to move forward

If you completed the reading and exercises in Chapters 2 and 3 of your notebook we hope that you have unplugged your mind *and* practised reflection and personal inquiry. You should have thought about your previous history and experience of mentoring (and how it made you think and feel). You should also have thought about the type of person you are and how your experience has shaped your perspective on your current situation. Knowing yourself (your likes, dislikes and motivations) can help you prepare and land with a positive impact in a new role.

If for any reason you have chosen to start your Notebook Mentor at this point, we encourage you to return to the exercises in Chapters 2 and 3 (even if you have completed them before). If you are determined to start here, please read on and embrace the challenges, questions and exercises we will be posing.

Flow

This chapter is broken down into a series of parts that share know-how and challenge your thinking regarding starting a new job. It is specifically segmented on the basis of time – before you start / your first 30 days / 30–90 days and 90 days and beyond. We suggest you complete your reflective practice and inquiry to these timelines. Try not to skip ahead and give yourself sufficient time to think about and process your experience. Where it makes sense we provide you with tools and focused development tips to help you manage your situation.

The chapter is broken down into the following parts:

Part 1   **Before you start**

Part 2   **The first 30 days**
Practical stuff
Listening and questioning
Your job profile
Your relationship with your line manager

Part 3   **30–90 days**
Assessing and managing priorities
Exploring and managing relationships
Impact and contribution
A word about line management

Part 4   **90 days and beyond**

Part 5   **Letting go of the past**
Being your best you

Part 1
Before you start

This Notebook Mentor assumes you have been offered the job! Congratulations – well done you!

Starting something new will likely mean getting down to business straight away. Many organisations (and books!) will encourage you to read and get prepared before you walk through the doors to the next thing. We recommend you be mindful. Getting ahead of the curve before you start might seem advantageous. Of greater benefit is putting work in to you. Allow yourself decompression time from what went before. Focus on getting physically prepared for the next thing. Catch up on sleep – let your mind process your previous experience. Eat well, exercise, get and stay hydrated. Not everyone can afford the money or time to have a holiday, however being refreshed and full of energy for the road ahead is certainly a worthwhile investment. Once you start the next thing, it will be a full-on ride.

If you are starting a new job in an organisation that is already familiar to you, then taking a break to allow yourself to see things with a fresh perspective is also a good idea. Letting go of pre-conceptions is likely to set you up better for having a high impact in your new role.

Give yourself an opportunity to focus on you by answering the following questions:

Building will and skill

◆ What are you thinking and feeling right now?

◆ What learning from your experience would you like to take forward into your new role? Is there anything you would like to leave behind?

◆ What personal goals would you like to work on? In this instance, we mean non-work goals. For example your health goals, relationship goals etc.) What small things can you commit to?

2
Part 2
The first 30 days

The first month in a new job is a great time for reflective practice and personal inquiry – doing lots of listening and asking lots of questions. This sounds straightforward enough, however, it's really easy to shift gear and get stuck in action mode – busily showing others that you know *how* to do the job!

Work hard at personal restraint – holding open the space for learning and allowing your brain time to absorb all the experience. Be open-minded and take the time to see things from multiple angles, building different perspectives. Doing this type of inquiry and active listening takes practice and can be quite exhausting. Done well it will help you land with impact and make faster decisions.

If you work in a big company there is every chance that you will be offered the opportunity to go through a **formal induction programme** – a session where you learn about the company, its goals and ambitions and perhaps the nature of your job within this context. This can be achieved many different ways such as via an on-boarding portal, through an e-learning module or training programme. It might happen before you start or anytime within the first six months of you joining (any later than this and you will probably have already formed your opinions that may be hard to shift). Don't be afraid to ask for an induction programme and grasp whatever opportunity you are offered with both hands, as it's an excellent way to practice the disciplines we have just been talking about.

Don't worry if you don't get to experience an induction though, as we have plenty of ideas about things for you to explore.

Practical stuff

Before we go deeper into the subject of listening, reflective practice and personal inquiry let's get some 30-day practical stuff out of the way. While it might seem a little bit pedestrian, we suggest you find out the following:

Tick them off when you think you have them sussed:

- [ ] Know the access points and layout of your workspace, office, workshop, retail store, collaboration site – whatever *the space* is
- [ ] Find out where key facilities are – toilets, coffee areas, the post and print room. If you work in multiple locations you'll likely build this knowledge over time
- [ ] If you travel a lot for work or work from home or a hot spot, ask people about when they meet face-to-face or how the company connects over technology
- [ ] Be aware of health and safety procedures in your workplace and make sure you get trained quickly if it's a requirement of your job
- [ ] Lookup any important conduct policies, rules or guidelines you might need to know (for example, you may need to complete Anti-Bribery Training or Anti-Fraud or Cyber Security Training to protect customer data)
- [ ] Ask someone to show you the basics of your company IT – for example how to log on to the company intranet, how to use IT remote access; mobile devices, cloud technology. If your job involves using Point of Sale (POS) systems or other customer management tools then chances are you'll be shown this as part of your induction
- [ ] If your company still uses them, find out how to work the landline desk phones and voicemail service.
- [ ] Check out access to any employee directory showing who your colleagues are and how to connect to them

☐ Many companies don't use Employee Handbooks anymore, but often have information on People or Human Resource (HR) Policy contained on the company intranet. This might give you access to important information like the Grievance Procedure or the Whistleblowing process

☐ If access is easy, try and experience the products and services that your company provide. It's probably easier to understand products sold in a fast food business, over say insurance products, however any opportunity to experience what your business does is time well spent.

NOTE

What if your company doesn't have these things?

If you work in a small start-up or franchise business your employer may not have some of the things mentioned above. Find out what useful information you can by asking other work colleagues or your line manager. Most companies, even very small ones have some kind of marketing material, online presence or social media account where you might find useful information.

In regards to your employment rights, these should be protected not only by your contract of employment but also by the governing employment laws of the country you live in. General information on your employment rights can always be found on government/state or other local specialist websites.

Use the blank pages of your Notebook Mentor to note down anything useful you might need to remember and add more notes to your 'Practical' list if you need to.

Listening and questioning

In your first 30 days, it's useful to build your understanding of what is expected of you in your job. Getting to know your new manager/department/organisation better will also help you get an early handle on how your job fits into the 'bigger picture'.

To do this you will need:

The role or job description that summarises what you are going to be doing (this includes the purpose of your job, the key deliverables and sometimes the skills, knowledge and attributes you need to be able to do the job well). Ask your People Team or HR Department for a copy of your job description (sometimes contained in something called a Job Family Framework). If no HR department exists then the next best person to ask is your line manager or the recruiter who helped you secure the job. If you haven't been provided with a job description start asking questions until you feel confident that you can fill out the following template.

Your job profile

◆ Job title:

....

◆ The purpose of my job is:

....

....

....

....

....

....

....

....

....

◆ The key deliverables in my job are:

◆ The skills, knowledge and/or qualifications I need to do my job are:

◆ The attributes (traits, abilities, style) I need to be successful in this job are:

For more information about job descriptions go to our website at
www.notebookmentor.com/resources

Sharing know-how

You've completed some useful inquiry and gained perspective on what it is you need to deliver in your new job. Take your time over the coming weeks to do the same research and inquiry into the following:

- The organisations' vision, mission, ambition or purpose
- Any company values that have been shared
- Financial targets and current performance (of the company, your division or department)
- The significant goals or objectives of the organisation – sometimes these can be long-term ambitions, at other times they are operating goals or annual targets
- How your job contributes to the company's ambitions

Take copious notes (in your physical notebook, electronically or by gathering additional files you can keep referring back to in your filing system or on a shared drive or via a collaboration zone).

And as you meet people remember to ask lots of open-ended questions. Here are some to get you started:

- How does the department/team operate?
- How do things work around here, the said and unsaid 'rules'?
- What are the hurdles or barriers to making this job a success?
- What's the culture like – how do I fit in?
- Who are the key people to influence to get the job done?
- How can I help you be successful in your role?
- How can you help me be successful in my role?
- Which other teams do we need to work with closely?

TIP
Don't limit your inquiry – talk to colleagues. Listen to the voices and opinions of others. Look online, read any accessible material. You don't need to process everything all at once. Let information sit with you – think it through. See what thoughts and feelings emerge.

Your relationship with your line manager

Think about your new boss! Establishing a positive and productive relationship with your new line manager is one of the most important things you can do in your new job.

All line managers are different and your new one might take some getting used to. Your line manager has probably invested time and effort to bring you on board. They most certainly are likely to want you to succeed. Don't be afraid to book plenty of time with them and make the most of their wisdom and insights. If you find your line manager remote or unavailable look for someone close to you who you interact with regularly and see if they are willing to give you time and advice.

Building will and skill

At the end of your first 30 days reflect on your data gathering and knowledge acquisition and answer the following questions:

◆ How does the job description or role profile match with your skills, experience and attributes? Are there any gaps – either additional things you need to build or additional things you have to offer?

◆ What are your key observations so far? This could be in respect to your job, your colleagues, the organisation's goals or purpose.

....

....

....

....

....

....

....

◆ What are you thinking and how you are feeling at this time?

....

....

....

....

....

....

....

◆ If you have been able to gain a sense of the company culture (its values, ways of working, unwritten rules, habits etc.) how do you think they are going to measure up against your values or principles?

◆ Has any information you have uncovered raised questions for you? If so, jot these questions down here:

- How can you get answers to these questions? Where can you find answers or who can help you with answers?

TIP

Don't worry if it takes you time to get answers to your questions or indeed if you end up having more questions as a result! Keep coming back to this section over the coming months and reflect on how your knowledge is changing and what new things you are learning.

Use the blank pages in this Notebook Mentor to record points from the key conversations you have each week so that you start to build a picture of your opportunities for success and your objectives.

Be bold, seek to follow up discussions and probe the people you meet with deeper conversation as you start to understand how things work and where the opportunities are.

Be aware of assumptions

In these initial discussions, it can be tempting to use all that experience and expertise that you've gathered in your previous roles to make swift judgements. Whilst you will need to pull all your thoughts together at some point and present your conclusions and plans to yourself and perhaps to others, in the initial stages it's often best to suspend judgement and to just listen and think.

Over your first 30 days, you can reflect on all your notes and put your previous knowledge and experience to work as you draw conclusions and formulate plans – but don't be in too much of a rush!

3

Part 3
30–90 days

The first month in a new job often flies by! While you are busy trying to keep an open, inquiring mind, no doubt your boss and the department you work in are all hoping you'll attend to that long action list that has been building for months before you even joined! Take heart – frenetic workplaces are nothing new – however, managing them does require you to apply some mindful thinking.

One useful strategy to employ in your second month in your new job is to look back over the first month and work out what you have been spending your time on. Make it a simple process by going through your historic diary and colour coding your time. Here is just one example of a colour-coding structure. Create one that fits with the nature of your work:

Green Time
Team time, 121's with colleagues, time with your manager

Blue Time
You time, space to reflect, inquire, process experience, learn and create

Red Time
Action time, on-the-job, doing your job activities

Orange Time
Others time, with customers, competitors and partners

Unless your role is specifically about serving customers directly or looking external to your company (Orange time), we suspect most of your time will be spent in the Green and Red time zones.

Congratulations if you are finding plenty of Blue time – it's often considered a luxury when in fact nothing could be further from the truth. Maintaining Blue time creates space for curiosity and innovation – things all companies need for successful teamwork and focused thinking. Keeping Blue time is notoriously hard work as we get settled in and busy! If you have the personal flexibility to do so, think about how you can balance your diary more evenly, finding time to reflect and work through problems at your own pace. Also, remember that ultimately we are all working in service of each other and our customers. Spending quality time considering the needs of others and of your customers *should* be a top priority for all of us!

An individual with a diary that is singularly loaded in one quadrant is heading for trouble. If you can balance the focus of your diary you will protect your health and well being and in the long-term this will benefit your employer much more than you getting burnt out quickly.

Assessing and managing priorities

By the time you've been in role 40 or 50 days, you should have more of a grasp on what your priorities are (the big things you must achieve to be successful) and the type of impact and contribution you can have.

If you are shaking your head at this point, noting your superiority in sussing it all out more quickly than our dreadfully long 50-day timeline, then remember the old saying of *pride coming before a fall*! We often form a quick judgement about what's urgent – as we'll see in a moment; this is different from working out what is important. It takes time to do both well!

If you want to change your life, change your diary

Building will and skill

Start by writing down all the things you think you need to achieve in your new job. If you can, as you go, group these things into clear and defined categories. For example, you might include categories like:

Operational activity or 'doing your job'
Using technology
Working with systems and processes
Planning
Customer management or experience
Supplier and partner relationships
Learning and Development

And if you are in a leadership or management role:

Strategy
Team leadership
Talent management
Performance management
Resource Planning
Capability development
These are just examples – find the categories that are right for you.

If you find this difficult, just list down all the things you have to do in your job. Once you have done this go back through the list and see if you can connect any related activity. If you prefer group things under a number or letter to show that they go together.

◆ Things I have to do in my job:

Here is an example for an IT Manager:

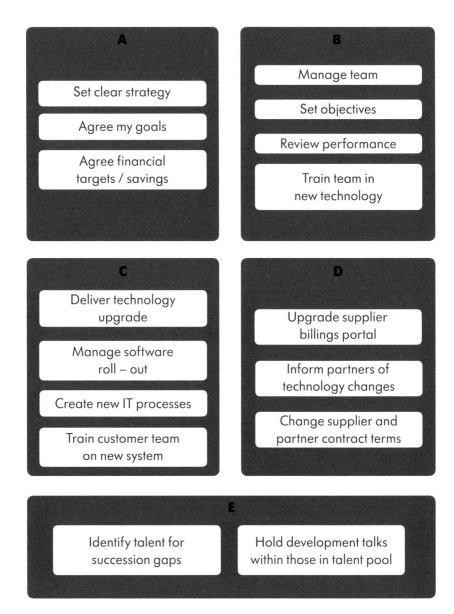

A
- Set clear strategy
- Agree my goals
- Agree financial targets / savings

B
- Manage team
- Set objectives
- Review performance
- Train team in new technology

C
- Deliver technology upgrade
- Manage software roll – out
- Create new IT processes
- Train customer team on new system

D
- Upgrade supplier billings portal
- Inform partners of technology changes
- Change supplier and partner contract terms

E
- Identify talent for succession gaps
- Hold development talks within those in talent pool

"Do your job and demand your compensation — but in that order"

Cary Grant

Once you have your action list and categories take a look at the four-box diagram on the following page. Take each grouping of activity (or a single activity if it stands on its own) and decide where it sits in one of the following four quadrants:

Top right quadrant – high urgency and high importance

Bottom right quadrant – high urgency but lower importance

Top left quadrant – high importance but lower urgency

Bottom left quadrant – lower importance and lower urgency

If you need to, work up a version of this on a large sheet of paper or a spreadsheet or in another digital form. The key is to keep thinking and moving your priorities around until such a time that you can start to see where things naturally lie.

If you like, seek the input of other colleagues or your line manager – however, remember this is as much about you getting your thinking straight, as it is about being told what the 'right answer' is. Our experience suggests there is no perfect answer because different stakeholders want different things. Listening to other people's views is great for collaboration, but applying your judgement is also very valid.

Higher Urgency

Higher Importance

Lower Importance

Lower Urgency

Taking these things into consideration, what priorities sit in the top right quadrant?

Note these down:

Top priorities that are both urgent and important

◆ 1 ....

....

....

◆ 2 ....

....

....

◆ 3 ....

....

....

◆ 4 ....

....

....

◆ 5 ....

....

....

Consider how you will address these challenges as well as those things that are being immediately demanded of you.

Exploring and managing relationships

Relationship Web

As you get through the first couple of months in your new job you'll start to understand the people you need to influence to help you be successful. You might also work out those people that could hinder you unless managed thoughtfully. A useful way to visually map these complicated networks and associations is to sketch out what we call a Relationship Web. The main difference between a Relationship Web and the more commonly known Stakeholder Map is that the latter is often more dedicated to understanding your stakeholders, and what their needs are above your own. A Relationship Web places you at the centre of multiple relationships and can help you answer a number of key questions:

- ☐ Who is someone *to* you? Are they a stakeholder, a team member, peer or manager, a distraction, a coach, a blocker, a source of information etc.?
- ☐ How do you need to influence them? What kind of relationship do you need to have with them? (Beyond let's assume, just a positive one)
- ☐ How often do you need to interact with them for you to influence them, or for them to help support you being successful?
- ☐ How critical are they to helping you achieve (or fail in) your objectives?

The diagram below shows a Relationship Web for Sarah, a Junior HR Manager who has just joined a mid-sized manufacturing firm.

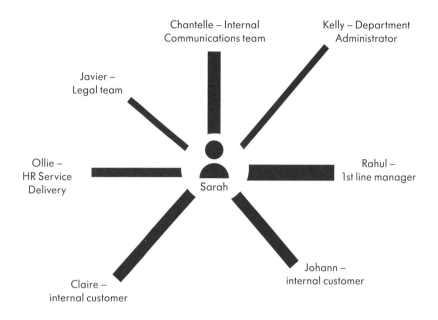

Comments on relationships

The **length of the line** denotes how much time Sarah needs to spend with each person or team. The **thickness** of the line denotes how critical the person or team is to helping Sarah achieve her objectives. Sarah has also made some comments about the nature of her relationships.

Rahul – based on the same floor. Good first impression. Feel like he can inspire me.
Johann – splits time between two sites. Hasn't had a positive experience with HR before. Seems to have a challenging style.
Claire – based on the same site. Keen to involve me.
Ollie – critical partner if I am to deliver for my customers. Seems nice but has a big workload.
Javier – only met briefly. Will need to get to know him but there isn't a pressing need at the moment.
Chantelle – seems ok but interdepartmental relationships between IC and HR seem strained.
Kelly – real workhorse. Also wants to help. Good source of knowledge as she has been here a long time.

Building will and skill

Using the pages here, or in the blank section of your notebook, create your first Relationship Web (we say first because we expect you to re-do this several times in your first year in your new role!)

◆ Who can help you be successful?

◆ Whose support do you need most to help you achieve your objectives?

◆ Who will you need to spend most of your time with?

◆ Who might get in the way of you succeeding?

◆ Who might be difficult to get on or deal with?

◆ What thoughts and feelings do you have about your relationship web?

◆ If you analysed and evaluated your relationship web what does it say about where you need to focus your immediate effort?

_____

_____

_____

_____

_____

_____

_____

◆ What conclusions do you draw about how you might use this insight?

_____

_____

_____

_____

_____

_____

_____

Impact and contribution

Now that you know a little more about your job, your line manager, the department and company you are working for and your top priorities, take a moment to think more deeply about what you want to achieve during your time in this job.

◆ What impact would you like to have in your job?

_____

_____

_____

_____

_____

◆ What do you hope to achieve – for yourself or others?

_____

_____

_____

_____

_____

_____

_____

_____

_____

◆ What are your fears (if any)?

◆ If you could be remembered for something in this new job – what would it be? It could be as simple as being remembered for being a great team player or it could be as complex as being remembered for leading the company through a period of significant transformation.

Sharing know-how

Having ambitions, hopes and fears is perfectly natural and logical. Articulating them when you start a new job can help if in the first few months you question the decision you made to take it on. It's not uncommon to feel differently about something as you settle in. Reminding yourself of why you made the decision in the first place will help you regain your equilibrium in the trickier moments that are more than likely to arise.

Being remembered for something may sound like a lofty ambition, but it is possible no matter your grade, job title or reward level. And setting out a goal like this can often keep you on your toes and ontrack, as you begin to get comfortable with what you are doing.

Your new colleagues may also ask you questions like these. It may be helpful if your answers don't just describe what you hope for yourself but recognise what is appealing to you about the new team, department and/or organisation you are joining. Your new colleagues will appreciate it and warm to you if you show that you genuinely want to be part of what they are working towards.

A word about line management

We've put this bit at the end because it won't apply to everyone who is starting a new role. If you are a line manager, you can incorporate your thinking from this section into the note pages in the previous sections.

Take a moment to carry out a situational assessment of your team. What do you want to learn during your first 90 days?

Your list might look something like the one below, but feel free to add other things to it.

- Who is in my team/first-line team?
- What is the background, character and experience of each team member?
- Do I have the necessary skills in this team to deliver what's required?
- Does this team act as a team? Are they a high performing team or are they still forming? Is there discord in the team?

- What's the state of morale and motivation in the team?
- How engaged and energised is each individual?
- Do I have the right resources to deliver what's needed (enough will and skill in the right places?)
- What do others say about members of the team or the team as a whole?
- Is the team organised in the best way it can be to deliver our goals?

Add your additional questions:

Think about where you can go for this information. Certainly, you should meet with your team members and find out more about them. You can also talk to your line manager and other colleagues who know your team. These people will have a view of your people but it's your job to draw your conclusions.

You will likely find that your team members want to talk to you. Some will want to discuss issues and concerns; others might want to make an early play for a promotion or a pay rise. Some may simply be checking you out. We all know that getting a new boss can be stressful so do take a moment to put yourself in the shoes of your team members and consider how they might be feeling about you coming on board. Consider what they need from you in these first 90 days and if you can provide it, do so.

There will always be some things you can't provide – for most line managers with a new team it takes time to establish whether you have the right players on the pitch so to speak, so you might not want to make any early commitments about job security or job moves before you have fully put together your plans (and had these signed off if needed). Managing your first 90 days with your new team is something of a balancing act. Yes, you do want to build relationships and rapport and you do want to get people on side. But you also want to reserve judgement until you know the way forward for everyone. This doesn't stop you doing the basics though, and you can still be warm, enthusiastic and friendly. Just remember to communicate – which is what your people will really want from you.

As you listen and research your team think about the key priorities. Great managers have a nose for focusing on the things that are most important and building out their plan from there.

Part 4
90 days and beyond

It's often said that the first three months of a new job is the time when you can see more of what is really going on than at any time that follows. You are not sullied by familiarity or bounded by expectation, fear or convention.

Use this freedom to make the most of noting down what you see and what you think is good or needs to change. At this stage it's not important that others share your views – it is simply your time to see this world unblinkered and raw. Whether you are right or wrong – this is your perspective at this moment.

◆ What do you see that is good and should be built upon?

◆ What do you see that is wrong, needs changing or is outdated?

Part 5
Letting go of the past

Have you ever worked with a new starter whose response to everything you discuss is to tell you what would have happened in their old job/old team? Have they also talked about their old team as 'we', even after they've worked with you in their new job for some time? Most colleagues forgive this for a while, you probably have yourself, but it can become wearing if it goes on. Your new colleagues will want you to put your energy in to the job you've now taken on and your new team. That's not to say that you shouldn't share your past experience. You should draw on examples from before, but with a focus on the new job and objectives.

If you find yourself still referring to your old colleagues as 'we' and you don't feel your new team is now your 'we' then take a moment to think why this might be?

◆ What's getting in the way of you feeling like you belong? Is there anything holding you back from jumping in with both feet?

◆ Have a think about how you might go about feeling more aligned with your new colleagues and increase your sense of belonging. Jot down some notes. Sometimes getting involved socially can help. Anything from a team lunch or joining in a sporting activity can deepen your relationships with colleagues as you get to know them better and find out different things about them, and they about you.

Being your best you

◆ Now that you have hopefully settled into your new role, this is a perfect time to take stock of your skills and your approach to work. Think about your experience and recent successes – what skills and working style did you employ to help you be successful?

....

....

....

....

....

....

....

....

◆ Now, consider those times when things didn't go so well. What reasons created this situation? Be honest about your skills, behaviour or working style – are there things you haven't fixed yet?

What might you still need to work on or change?

....

....

....

◆ Finally have a good, hard think about the new job. Consider the context in which you are working – the people, the organisation and its goals. What skills, behaviours and working style will be most crucial in this role?

Hopefully, you'll see that many of your skills and traits will be useful to you in the new job. However, you may find that there are gaps too. That's fine and is only to be expected, after all, many of us move roles to stretch ourselves and do something new. The key is to have a plan for how you will build those extra skills that you're going to need. You can discuss this with your new boss or your HR representative if you have one. Or you might find our other Notebook Mentors helpful.

Hardly anyone excels at everything and your time is going to be precious in the next few months so it's probably best to prioritise any development needs that might directly impact on your new role. You can do this in Chapter 5 of this notebook in the section on Personal Development Planning.

For now, list out any priority development gaps you have:

Last thoughts

So, that's about it. Lot's for you to think about in these first 90 days but with the help of Notebook Mentor, you should be well prepared and effective!

Remember to keep an eye on your health and wellbeing, to keep checking in on your emotional state and to acknowledge that being new brings extra stresses. Why not make a final few notes below on where you can go in the next few months for support, comfort, confidence or whatever you need to help you through.

From everyone at Notebook Mentor, we wish you good luck!

Let your curiosity get the better of you

5

Chapter 5

Applying your learning

"Learning never exhausts the mind"

Leonardo da Vinci

What have you learnt?

If you have managed to work through part of *or* this entire Notebook Mentor, then congratulations! As a minimum you have:

- Put quality time into thinking about yourself and your situation
- Developed self-awareness and a deeper understanding of who you are
- Applied the skills of reflection, inquiry, restraint, perspective and judgement in response to managing a moment that matters to you
- Given your brain downtime to process your experience
- Enhanced your creativity and problem-solving skills

You may also have:

- Learnt something about yourself that enables you to make decisions or take action regarding your situation
- Enhanced your knowledge, know-how, skills or attributes
- Developed deeper relationships with others

Building will and skill

◆ Write down your thoughts and feelings on your learning from this experience? Was the experience positive? What was hard or easy about the Notebook Mentor approach? What would you like to have done more or less of?

◆ If you found the experience challenging, difficult or frustrating, why might this be? How could Notebook Mentor support you differently or more effectively through this moment? What do you conclude from this experience?

Please do let us know your feedback on our mentoring approach. You can leave your feedback on our website at **www.notebookmentor.com**

What might you do next?

In Chapter 3 of the notebook under the title 'the so what factor' we suggested that the experience of working through this book is an end in itself – it is the practice of reflection, inquiry, restraint, perspective and judgement that is as useful as a passion for action! As you know we firmly believe in the benefits of this time investment in you. However, we also suspect that our partnership in challenging and guiding you through this mentoring experience will have stimulated thoughts and ideas about things you want to do. If this has happened this is also a great outcome.

Before we end this Notebook Mentor we would, therefore, like to prompt you to consider:

- Any actions you might like to take
- Reflection on any actions you have taken already
- How your learning could be consolidated into a Personal Development Plan (PDP) or development review
- How to continue your multi-sensory learning, connecting your experience to a related activity or new experiences

Actions you might like to take

As with performance management philosophies make these actions S.M.A.R.T. (Specific, Measureable, Achievable, Relevant and Timely). Here are some examples of S.M.A.R.T. actions:

1. Arrange a meeting with my line manager in the next 2 weeks to discuss my Personal Development Plan.
2. In the next week write 'my story' using the information generated in this notebook. Use this to prepare for the job interview I have in 3 weeks.

If you struggle with writing S.M.A.R.T. objectives don't dismiss your ideas or thoughts – they are still very relevant and worth noting down and getting on with. For example, you might come up with an action such as 'listen more and get to know my boss better'.

It may not be a S.M.A.R.T. action but it is a worthy pursuit. You can work on your action planning skills as time goes on.

Actions

- ◆
- ◆
- ◆
- ◆
- ◆
- ◆
- ◆
- ◆
- ◆

- ....
  ....

- ....
  ....

- ....
  ....

- ....
  ....

- ....
  ....

- ....
  ....

- ....
  ....

- ....
  ....

- ....
  ....

Reflection on actions already taken

If you have already taken a number of actions as you worked through the notebook, create some space to reflect on how these actions played out.

Action:

Others response to action:

Thoughts and feelings about the outcome of any action:

What you conclude or might do differently in the future?

Action:

Others response to action:

Thoughts and feelings about the outcome of any action:

What you conclude or might do differently in the future?

Action:

Others response to action:

Thoughts and feelings about the outcome of any action:

What you conclude or might do differently in the future?

Personal development planning

Writing a Personal Development Plan or completing a more informal development review, is another way of prioritising what you might want to do next to build on the learning experience. It can be written any way you want (perhaps your company has a standard proforma?). Here is a list (though not exhaustive) of things worth including:

Your name

....

Your job title

....

The date

....

Your key development objectives (this might include building on strengths or closing gaps. You might want to use a skill more or build your knowledge, develop a trait or attribute, grow your network, work on a relationship or a change in your mindset)

The activities you must undertake to achieve your objective (this might include reading, a training course, practice on the job, listening to someone you admire, talking to a colleague.)

The outcome of your development (for example, if you developed your network what might it look like in six months? What does 'good' look like?)

Any support you may need (from your line manager, your partner, another colleague)

Any resources you may need (financial investment for a training course, time, others support)

Timing (when the development action needs to take place or over what time period)

You can find a downloadable Personal Development Plan Proforma on the Notebook Mentor website by going to
www.notebookmentor.com/resources

Consolidating your learning

When working through a meaningful experience there is every chance it will affect or connect to something else going on in your life. Exciting, challenging or dramatic events often have this radiating impact on you and those around you.

Notebook Mentor believes in the value of supported mentoring for tackling these meaningful experiences especially if you can define them with some sense of completeness – like 'starting a new job' or 'becoming a manager'. Tackling these moments by thinking of them as a single challenge can have an encouraging and positive impact on your ability to take control of them and not feel overwhelmed by the situation.

Of course, we also recognise that there is little in life that is completely clear-cut and neatly compartmentalised. Meaningful experiences can be complex and ambiguous, with no timeline or a messy array of things that have to be dealt with simultaneously.

This means there is great merit in taking your learning from one particular 'experience' and using it to build your will and skill to apply to other challenges. It is also useful in times when things seem to be happening together. For example:

Perhaps you want to get to know yourself better because you are struggling in some of your relationships.

Perhaps you have suffered a serious illness and this has entirely changed your perspective on what you want from your career.

Perhaps you have just become a manager for the first time and you are faced with needing to restructure and downsize your team.

Perhaps you have just returned from maternity leave and have been asked to work on strategy as a leader of a complex project.

Here are some tips on how to consolidate your learning from this mentoring experience and apply it to a connected activity or something completely new.

Sharing know-how
Mind mapping

You may be familiar with mind mapping (remember the work of Tony Buzan?) Don't worry if you are not. There's lots of great reading material out there and some excellent TED Talks on the subject. Have a look at our resources page for more information by going to **www.notebookmentor.com/resources**.

Mind mapping is a very popular *visual* and *kinaesthetic* learning technique that helps you organise and remember things. For Notebook Mentor users we hope it can help you learn, store, and retrieve information that is important to you regarding a meaningful experience. Equally, we think it might help you access what you already know, such that you can take your acquired learning and apply it to a new or related challenge.

In everyday situations, mind mapping is often used when taking notes (at a seminar, in a lecture, in a team meeting). Rather than writing a transcribe of the conversation, however, it is about capturing keywords, ideas or pictures in such a way that when you look at them again they trigger a memory of what was most important.

We think it's a brilliant technique for thinking through a meaningful experience to you – free-associating with that moment and working out exactly what is going on. This means key thoughts; feelings, information, memories and ideas that are in your mind are captured on paper. Think of your mind map as the branches and roots of a tree – separate but connected.

Let's try it out.

- Start with a blank sheet of paper turned on its side (landscape rather than portrait).
- Think about the experience you are going through. Write the name of this experience in the centre of the page. (You can use a visual metaphor for the experience if you'd prefer).
- Using your pen (or different coloured pens if you like) build out your mind map free form, capturing key ideas/phrases or words on different branches or roots. If sub-ideas come to mind, connect them to the main branch to which they relate.

- Sit with your thoughts, allowing your mind to process your experience or thinking. Come back to it if necessary.

For argument's sake let's say that the experience you are going through is 'the first 90 days in my new job'. Many significant ideas, feelings, pieces of information and actions could be related to this experience (as shown in Figure 1.0.).

> **NOTE**
> This mind map is a simple word based picture. Hopefully this will help you understand the process in its simplest form. Use pictures, colour and graphics to make it even more memorable and remember that you can now use mind mapping Apps if you prefer to work digitally. We recommend pen and paper!

Don't worry if you tried the technique on the exact same topic and your picture looks completely different! Mind maps are unique things – it's a reflection of what matters to you. By writing out your mind map you have neatly organised and summarised what is most important to this particular moment. You have created a visual picture of key ideas that link to much more detailed information – already stored in your brain, or waiting to be discovered and learnt!

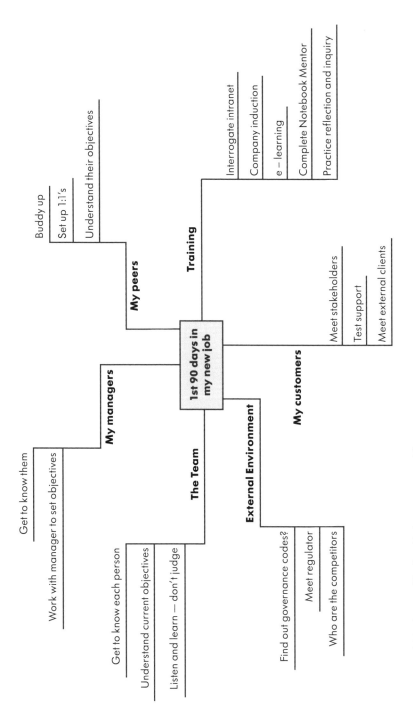

Figure 1.0. Mind map – "The first 90 days in my new job"

Reflecting and connecting further

Let's say that one of the reasons you are starting a new job is that in your previous job you fell out with a number of your co-workers and decided to leave the organisation. You are determined that no matter who was to blame, you want to avoid this situation happening again. Now (as shown in Figure 2.0.) your web reshapes with new ideas, connections and implications.

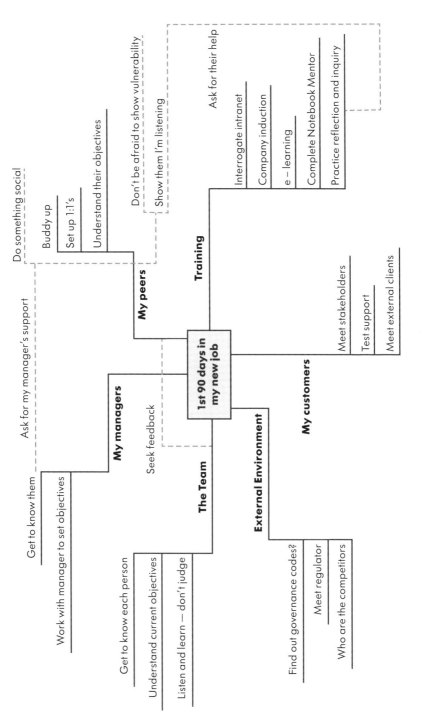

Figure 2.0. Mind map – "Getting on with co-workers and the first 90 days in my new job"

By visualising these connections you can see how they relate to one another as well as determine if something additional needs working on. You are clear about what you need to do – plus you have a checklist of sorts to come back and measure progress against.

Summary

Sometimes creating your mind map will be straightforward – at other times you might feel you are knitting spaghetti! Don't worry – it doesn't have to follow an immediate logic to be useful. Often when you've jotted down information once, more connections will appear if you do another version of the mind map a second or third time. Keep going with it as it becomes easier with practise.

Building will and skill

Take the subject of this Notebook Mentor and create a mind map for all the connected thoughts, key ideas, learning and action it has sparked.

Is there a related experience connected to this moment? If so, build on or create a new mind map that brings the information together.

Your mindmap:

Your mindmap:

Other sources of support

Notebook Mentor is <u>only one</u> of many sources of guidance and support.

The Internet contains a vast amount of information and is an *access* point to knowledge, wisdom and practical experience. It is because of this that it is both hugely powerful *and* time-consuming and complex. By all means, use what you are familiar with – but don't be afraid to do some research and give something new a go – just as you have done here.

At Notebook Mentor we are keen for you to unplug (at least a little) from your digital devices and blend your learning experience. This is why you can only buy our books in physical form. We want to encourage you to allow your brain the space to process experience and build skill in kinaesthetic reflective practice.

We also suggest you look for ways to share experience in the physical presence of others. By all means use the Internet to connect to people who might be liked minded, inspiring and of interest – but try and get out and meet other people face to face. Be brave and reach out to others and ask for help. There is generally someone in the workplace that is decent and human enough to lend you an ear or provide a helping hand. Chatting to someone you don't know at work event might be scary at first. Asking someone to share their wisdom and knowledge might seem daunting. Be thoughtful, respectful and brave. Use your judgment and instinct to determine the motive for helping you. If it is honourable or benign then why not give it a go.

If you need more help with the work or career experience you are going through, reach out to other obvious places like your family and friends. If it is affecting your health or other aspects of your wellbeing, talk to your doctor, a counsellor or qualified health practitioner. Look to local government offices, community support groups, charities and local education services.

Be kind to yourself

And remember to be kind to yourself – do not expect to progress, change or resolve everything in one sitting. More often than not it takes time and patience.

Remember to visit our website **www.notebookmentor.com** for regular updates and additional resources.

References and acknowledgements

Chapter 3
Goleman, D. PhD., (1998), 'What Makes a Leader' in *Harvard Business Review*, November – December, p.88

Chapter 5
Buzan, T. (2002) *How to MindMap®*, Harper Collins Publishers

Disclaimer

Further Reflection

.